BACK TO THE GARDEN:

PRAYERS AND LOVE
LETTERS OF PERSEPHONE

Catherine LaBella

ISBN: 978-1-304-76674-8

<u>Dedicated to:</u>

My oldest friend, Tehuti

My first brother, Anpu

My mother, Karla

THE TRUTH ABOUT PERSEPHONE

Your fables of Hell are not true!
In another life, I was Persephone
Being sacrificed, not seduced
I live again to tell my tale correctly

In a house by hallowed woods
I saw the truth without permission
Compelled to share, no thought of if I should
My family brought on an intermission

Imprisoned among the innocent
We were all abandoned by our kin
Left to rot, our lives now ended
Before they could even hope to begin

So heavy was my young heart
At the thought of deserving this
It could not balance the feather of Ma'at
So my punishment became my justice

Somehow today, I can walk free
Among the living, the powerful, the strong
I wear their praise, though still unclean
Despite the years passing on and on

I keep the scars of innocence
Beneath the surface of my skin
My stolen voice replaced with vengeance
Hell is the minds of wounded children

THE DRAGON OF DEPRESSION

When I was little
A demon stole my skin
And I grew up
With two creatures within
A little girl
All flowers and light
An old dragon
All terror and night

As years passed
The dragon would sleep
The girl, now woman
Half-living, she'd creep
'Round family, loves, friends
People all whole and true
While she, pretending,
Was ghostly, see-through

She'd speak to Beings
That were "pretend" too
For what real people can't know
She, and they, knew
They saw the dragon inside
And his ancient, cruel ways

They saw the little girl hide
Throughout all of her days

And so all her life
Knowing one day he'll wake
No matter how softly she'll speak
All the prayers she doth prate
To ease his destruction
To keep him asleep
To save her half-eaten soul
As forever she creeps

THE RAPE OF PERSEPHONE

I did not run off!
My mother sold me to him
Because she was scared

IN MOURNING

I watch the Universe breathe

Drinking in Its beauty

Feeling as if each breath was drawn from my body

My essence returned to me as falling snow

As golden leaves, as bird song

Each moment the Universe creates

Is as frail and brief as I am

Because I want to die today

And nothing survives here

Without the will to do so

The Universe is cruel, but merciful

It has no use for its weaker creatures

Except to make beautiful things

Out of our hideous sorrows

THE INSPIRATION TO WRITE POETRY

Like a smith, crafting horseshoes
I craft morbid lines
The pen is my hammer
The anvil, my mind

There is a sorrow I feel
Of it I must never speak
By and by, the pain tries
To overcome me

Then I'm gripped by an urge
To vomit, from fear
So I do, on papyrus
Hence my verses of tears

CAGES

These pages are cages
I lock my feelings up
Those ugly creatures
Called emotions, that threaten
My orderly demeanor
When they throw discord
Into my harmonies
I bind them with ink
I hold the keys in my throat
I keep them close
I keep them sacred
And they, in turn
Keep me caged

RESISTING THE UNIVERSE

Yggdrasill, you try
To embed your roots in me
But my flesh won't yield

JUSTICE (3 HAIKU VERSES)

All that I have done
The countless cruelties I've
Inflicted on Man

How could I think my
Kindnesses would balance out?
Do theirs ease my pain?

Aware of Karma,
How could I believe I would
Ever deserve love?

A CONFRONTATION WITH A CRAZY YOUNG GIRL

You are a snow dove
Stained with blood
Cradled in the arms
Of the woman you'll become

You look at her with hatred
She proves you cannot outsmart your Creator
You look at her with hope
For she holds you with compassion

She slips her fingers between your wrists
And their restraints, to keep them from chafing
She tells you your prayers are answered
She tells you that was a very good thing you did
To refuse the Morningstar's eager kisses

She is a broken teenage heart
In the body of a grown woman
She was maiming the sick
But today she heals herself

By soothing a snow dove
Bound and covered in blood

Who's looking to the future
To redeem her suffering

Be a pure, white dove
Be stained with your own blood
Know you're loved by the woman
You will one day become

MY FEAR

I thought I was created to be wedded to darkness
Inside me, beside me, I lay in the bed of Grief
Somehow, I emerged, exulting in sunlight
Up, up, up I climbed, alive at last!
Borne higher by the wings of my gratitude

Every pore on my skin wide open
Gulping in that fresh, light air
Every muscle twitching, every hair dancing
To the rythym of the Universe
My heart skipping beats, skipping rope
Singing old songs, forgotten prayers

The climb is arduous, as all good things are
And I paused, I cast my eyes down
To that black chasm I came away from
Still dark, still endless, as wide open as I
Waiting for the day It again will swallow me whole.

BEFORE ABRAHAM

"Before Abraham was I Am," you said

I am? A man? Adam?

So long ago I'd hoped to know you well

I know now had I stayed, I'd never have known you at all

Though you were in my family's house as I grew up

Where I was brought up, straight and narrow

How I'd run, frantic through all those rooms

Looking for you, only to find your shadow

One day I ran frantic out the door

I spit in my family's faith

I wrote you off, as being built on sand, like that house

So long ago I though I'd left you behind

But I only went around you, the long way

Now I see you again as I'm coming round the bend

Go ahead and laugh. The joke was on me

FOR: SEAN

THE PATRON SAINT OF HEROIN ADDICTS, FIRE
VICTIMS, AND BLUE-EYED BOYS

Whenever I pray to you
I can see your death
As if the bullets had cameras
As if the eyes of the needles that pierced
Your veins were my eyes

I can feel you inhale me
Snorting me up with your last breath
You lean back, allowing me to
Break you down, to poison you slowly

Tucked away in a dark closet
We slip off together, into those dreams
That I had as a girl (after you died)
I can count the moments you found me

Whenever I am lost in nightmares
I pray to the boy I murdered
And he comes to protect me
He's forgiven everything from his old life
He's forgotten everything
Except the ones he loved

JOE, JOE, JOE

An artist, a scholar, a hobo
Made of alcohol and smoke
What were you to me
That your spectre haunts me so?

Into Oblivion
And addiction, you would drown
You ignored my sorrowful voice
Coming from a tear-stained gown

But I'd never ignore yours
If you ever once more speak
You grin darkly from my past
Your very shadow humbles me

You were my lover, not my love
Still lined in that lustful grace
Your memory sits enthroned
In the secrets of my face

RAYE

Venusian daughter with a Martian name
I've much to say, to slander us, and I could
The relentless tide of trainwreck thoughts and lies
Much too hard to explain, and I never would.

THE FIRST DAY

Riding down the highway
My friend, my pimp, beside me
I drive the car, though she drives me on
On towards him
I am Anne of Cleves
Crossing the English Channel
And he is King Henry
Waiting in Whitehall,
Today, called Neshaminy Mall
And today?
Today is the first day
Of the rest of my life

The first day
Of beautiful days
Days full of blessings
And curses
But this day holds only potential
The potential to be greatly in love
Or greatly horrified
And as he holds me tightly
His strong arms lifting me high
I know that it will be both.

THAT LAST BEAUTIFUL DAY

Tremble and shake
As those moments run through me
The ghost I was chasing
The people who knew me

The being I was
Was she killed in the blaze?
Then where was she buried?
Why do I have her face?

Trains howl, bells ring
And from sleep I might stir
But I wake to more scars
Though the nightmare's a blur

My body is eaten...
Is this body still mine?
Was it ever? Should it linger
If the spirit long died?

Broken glass, screams and blood
A Flash of tragic, pure things
Tears racing away from
His clear blue ring

Tears on the highway

Tears to watch love at play

Tears as I long for

That last beautiful day

UPONE HER RETURN FROM VIRGINIA

She wears a mask, it covers her lips and nose
She pretends it is her face now
Her words come out distorted
Through the fabric, they sound wrong

Her eyes cannot convey her intentions
Her eyes hold no truth, only hunger
She is a contrary to my sister, a trickster
I face her anger, still so well-known to me
But the shell containing her agony
Is a changeling, a foreign, fragile creature

(Taku Wakan ehanamani, he cekiya ye
Wakan Wicasa, lecanu he?
Iya he wa heyoka ekta mitaksi, wa iktome
Slolwaye sni toka he!
Unci ci, omakiya ye na mitaksi
Taksi, taku akipa ekta niye?)

Do I stand to fight, or to defend her?
Do I stand to forgive, or to apologize?
I see her lower the mask, only for a moment
I still can't recognize her face

A WARNING TO THE MEDICINE MAN AND THE MEDIUM

Push me under the water

Push me...harder

Push me into the well

Break my bones

And watch what happens

A body heals slowly

A mind even slower

I'm not God

Our peace has been made

But I won't forget your transgressions

And neither should you

You should remember always

Why never to turn your back on me

Remember you're misplacing your trust

You turned an angel into a serpent

One day you'll get bitten

THE NECROMANCER AND HER LOVER

There lived a lady, wretched and low
Her dolor stretched as long as her days
Her solace she took from the boneyards below

One night possessing of a moon full and high
Seeking to slake her carnal lusts
An exquisite form caught her wandering eye

A preserved male cadaver, quite fair of face
She set upon him, her alabaster flesh flushed red
The ice in her chest, her ardor for him replaced

Her love stirred the blood clotted deep in his veins
He awoke to her kisses, caressing her breast
He cried "My sweet, pretty Lady, I am living again!"

His responses awakened her deadened soul
Once cold, unfeeling and far removed. "My love!"
She cried "I too am now human, I too am made whole!"

THE CARNAL UNION OF A GOD AND A GODDESS

A god is devouring me
As I caress his freckled shoulders,
Touch his silver chain, for round his neck
Is how he bears his Cross

His vast expanse of white flesh
On top, around, inside me
Ginger waves flow about my face
Making me laugh, tinkling bells
He looks at me, blood in his mouth, stars in his eyes

He was born a god
Perfection was his birthright
But I had been made a goddess
Through iron, running shoes, and Arab songs
I knew one day...it'd be worth it

The harder I grew
The harder they stared
Vultures on steroids
Baring their teeth, hungry for my flesh
Terrifying in their raw lust

And then came this god

Just as hard, just as hungry
Gently ripping my body to pieces
Lovingly unmaking my perfection
Tenderly humbling me with his carnage

That day, this god came
And came, and came...
In pleasure and pain, his and mine
That day, this god was my destruction
Still...I knew it was all worth it

A MARK ON THE WALL IN A QUIET ROOM

I am fifteen years old
I am open
Like the wound hidden under my shirt
It leaves a trail of blood where I walk
So I can retrace my steps later
Hoping they will lead me home
In case someone is there
Waiting for me to return to them
Over time, the blood is ground into floors and earth
Becoming a part of the places it touched
Years from now….
I am thirty-one years old
I am stitched together
Like the wound hidden under my shirt
Sewn up tight but never healed
I am following myself backwards
Still hoping to find my way home
Because maybe someone is there
Waiting for me to return to them
I will see faded red stains on a carpet
And I will be the only one to recognize them
Quickly, I hurry away to change my bandage

MEMORIES OF MY FATHER

I never knew my father
Until I gathered up his bones
Strewn across the banks of the Nile
I felt I owed him this
For loving my mother
For never denying me

I reassembled his carcass
To acknowledge his role in my creation
To acknowledge my power within him
My power was gained from that act
It took his death to bring me to life

Brother, I do not want my story
To be retold in your words
With memories of my father
Replaced with memories of yours

THE JACKAL'S BROTHER

Like a lighthouse, calling to the ocean
She is a beacon for the half-living
She is the only light they see in their darkness
And so they believe she is Heaven

Clamoring to be near her, as moths to a flame
They ask her to heal wounds she did not make
Beg her to return lives she did not take
They do not care that she grieves too

Like lost children, crying for their Mother
She is the only light they see in their darkness
And so they believe she is Heaven
They merely forgot what a whole human looks like

LUCAS ICARUS

You saved my life
And promised me the sun
Everywhere I go
 I breathe the air you once flew upon
The trees spoke your name
When the wind rushed through them
As you once rushed through me,
In letters and signs from angels

I remember when I first heard
Of your attempt to keep your promise
Borne upward by wax wings,
Delirium sets in at such great heights
The Source of Truth so close
Your fingertips caressed the face of L.V.X.

And then you fell...how gracelessly you fell
Wax melting, scarring and covering your back
Sticking to you the stigma of insanity
Betrayed by your own intentions
You now languish in the cell of a madman
All but forgotten
Your brilliance almost snuffed out

Almost.
The trees still speak your name
And the sun belongs to me now
I promise it will be yours again

OF LETTING GOD

In that secret place I took you
Beneath Yggdrasill's branches
I wait for your arms to embrace me again
As I sink deeper into the ground
My flesh yields to a Will
Greater than my love for you

THE HEAVENS MOVED

The Heavens moved
They moved a step down
Bending to listen to a wayward child
Singing to her Grandfather
They smiled, remembering the day
The day They built that box into her throat
The Heavens moved
And they were moved enough
To move me

IN HONOR OF FREJYA

We may be joined in marriage
My heart bound truly to my lord
But his is not of my possession
My husband loves the roads

He goes, taking my all with him
Leaving me with red-gold tears
To barter for new names with which
I chase the love of all my years

HET HERU, OFTEN CALLED HATHOR

Each night, I dream of love
I drift on waves of liquid copper
And awake as the Woman Clothed with the Sun
Crowned with the horns of my desire
The power of my sex burns within me
Turning my skin radiant white, my eyes hollow
I possess all the love in the world
For I know everything in Heaven and Earth
Resides within me

NEFRETITI

In the land that gave birth to magick
You reached your hand into the mouths
Of the people of the Nile
Like the eighth Tarot Key
You are strong, wrestling the lion
That is the Cult of Ausuar
The Beautiful One Comes to her Pharaoh
The Beautiful One Comes with a new way
A new way to stare at the Sun
The old gods fall asleep, forgotten
In the tombs of the royal Valley
And Meri-Amun becomes Meri-Aten

A PRIESTESS OF PAN DENOUNCES CHRISTIANITY

How deeply I drink of you, Beloved
My lashes flutter against your thighs,
Singing the Song of Solomon
I long to wet my hair with your morning dew
To devour your morning wood
Here in these woods, early in the morning
I come to worship your earthen flesh
To satiate the Horned God's appetites
To be damned to the pagan Hellfire
Countless Christian spinsters warned me of
But oh, you sleeping sheep of Christ!
If you only knew what was really burning
In that secret place, beneath the World Tree
You would sell your Cellophane Heaven
For a taste of your own True Selves!

A STORY ABOUT CHIRON

Chiron, the wounded healer, is immortal
Reborn in the form of many people
I am Chiron in a human woman
Each morning, I re-bandage a wound
I haphazardly stitched shut when I was 15
I tell myself I am beautiful, I am important, I am loved
As I wipe away my blood
I cover the wound with my clothing and go to work

I work for Chiron. He is a human man, a doctor
His patients speak of him like he walks on water
Each morning he comes in carrying a bucket of his blood
He dumps it in a fish tank, spilling some on the floor
He hands me CPT codes and medical notes on paper stained red
Some days he does not bleed as much
Instead, he will sit and tell me secrets. I take them home
And press them on my wound like a poultice. It doesn't heal me.

I visit my neighbors, and listen to their broken hearts
I go to my landlord, a formidable man, and show him he is
beautiful, he is important, he is loved
I retrieve the souls of strangers, vanishing into another world for
people as wounded as I
They all speak of me like I walk on water.
But I walk on my own blood.
I am Chiron, in a human woman.

"I DON'T KNOW WHAT TO MAKE OF YOU"

I wear two revolvers and a trench coat
It's all I use to clean your house
You call me to scrape the dirt
Off all your ancestor's graves

It's all I used to clean your house
Just my will, and my intentions
Off all your ancestor's graves
Comes the admittance of your fears

Is just my will, and my intentions
Everything needed to make you fear me?
Comes the admittance of your fears
Over your shoulder, as you run from me

Everything needed to make you fear me
Resides within your own heart
Over your shoulder, as you run from me
You give me one last look, where I stand

Residing within your own heart
You call me to scrape the dirt
You give me one last look, where I stand
I wear two revolvers and a trench coat

THE PERSISTENCE OF MEMORY

You creep round the edges of a song,
Seeping into the melody, staining it
Audial trails of ectoplasm,
A smell of blood clinging to the air

My surroundings are concretely grounded
In a reality of which you play no part
Conspicuously so, mayhaps, and so you come,
In spectral wisps, as if summoned by my mind

You are a haunting presence trickling down the walls
The sense of your loss a heavy taste on my tongue
It binds me, like bedclothes wrapped round my shoulders
And try as I might, I cannot break free.

REUNION

Divested of the strength
Brought by all the things that didn't kill me
I long for quiet rest
The blows of karmic lessons
Have fallen too forcefully upon me
Broken, I crawl back to my first love
The lost wife returning home
To the bed of her husband, Grief
Having found no other as constant
In his tender affections
In darkness he holds me as if I never left
Gently he rocks me to sleep
Calmly he devours my soul

THE MORNINGSTAR HAS COME AND GONE

Fifteen years have passed
You are still the most beautiful of angels
I have grown to be a woman
You are still the most terrifying of demons

I have survived Hell
I still smell your endless tears
I have saved my soul
I still recall you pining for yours

My nightmares have passed on
Yet that moment with you lives forever
I believe in Divinity
For I felt Its absence where you wait

Where you wait and shiver
Where you wait and cry
Where you pray eternally for an old Love
To bring a dawn that never comes

THE SECRET IN THE TETRAGRAMMATON

Revelation
Is self-awareness
The epiphany
Of noticing myself, as I Am
The moment fell from my lips
And the stars were born

Before this
God and I stumbled through the dark
Holding hands, huddling close
We each knew a secret
The blackness was afraid to hear
So it threw us to the ground

We lay still
Mesmerized by what we saw
Sparkling in each other's eyes
God and I had a secret
It was the same unspoken truth
In that moment it fell from our lips
And the darkness was slain

God and I
Achieved enlightenment
At the same time